STUDEBAKER TRUCKS
1927-1940
PHOTO ARCHIVE

STUDEBAKER TRUCKS
1927-1940
PHOTO ARCHIVE

By Howard L. Applegate

Iconografix
Photo Archive Series

Iconografix
PO Box 609
Osceola, Wisconsin 54020 USA

Library of Congress Card Number 95-77494

ISBN 1-882256-40-9

95 96 97 98 99 00 5 4 3 2 1

Cover and book design by Lou Gordon, Osceola, Wisconsin

Printed in the United States of America

Book trade distribution by Voyageur Press, Inc. (800) 888-9653

PREFACE

The histories of machines and mechanical gadgets are contained in the books, journals, correspondence and personal papers stored in libraries and archives throughout the world. Written in tens of languages, covering thousands of subjects, the stories are recorded in millions of words.

Words are powerful. Yet, the impact of a single image, a photograph or an illustration, often relates more than dozens of pages of text. Fortunately, many of the libraries and archives that house the words also preserve the images.

In the *Photo Archive Series*, Iconografix reproduces photographs and illustrations selected from public and private collections. The images are chosen to tell a story—to capture the character of their subject. Reproduced as found, they are accompanied by the captions made available by the archive.

The Iconografix *Photo Archive Series* is dedicated to young and old alike, the enthusiast, the collector and anyone who, like us, is fascinated by "things" mechanical.

1927 estate car with caning.

INTRODUCTION

Studebaker's history with commercial vehicles began in 1852 when two brothers, Henry and Clem, opened a South Bend, Indiana blacksmith shop where they specialized in the building of horse drawn wagons. Soon, three other brothers, John Mohler, Jacob and Peter joined the family firm that evolved into the Studebaker Brothers Manufacturing Company. They became famous as builders of Conestoga wagons used in the Westward movement. They also built working vehicles for farmers and some buggies and traps for non-commercial use. During the American Civil War, the Studebakers manufactured wagons for the Union army. Studebaker exhibited a full range of products at the 1876 Centennial in Philadelphia and in the 1880's and 1890's had a reputation for making reliable wagons and quality carriages. Business historians believe Studebaker to have been the world's largest producer of horse drawn vehicles.

The brothers were slow to recognize that motor vehicles permanently would replace horse drawn equipment, so they entered the automotive market cautiously and late. Starting in 1902, they made and sold small electric cars and in 1904 began to sell cars made for them by the Garford company of Ohio. A few of the electrics and Garfords were converted into commercial units. The electrics were built in the 1902-1912 era while one-off of the gas powered Garfords were made through 1910. In 1908, Studebaker Brothers bought into the E-M-F Corporation and by 1909 controlled that Detroit-based company. The products of E-M-F during the 1908 through 1912 period included the EMF 30 and the Flanders 20. Some of the Flanders vehicles were manufactured as half-ton panel delivery units. In 1911, the Studebaker Brothers merged E-M-F into their own company, which was reorganized as the Studebaker Corporation.

In 1913, Studebaker officially entered the truck field by marketing three-quarter-ton delivery vehicles in panel or express versions. A bus model was added to the lineup in 1915. During World War One, Studebaker received a government contract for military ambulances built on the delivery vehicle chassis. The civilian light duty trucks were made and sold through 1917, when the truck factory was converted to military production. For some unexplained reason, after World War I, Studebaker dropped the commercial vehicle range. The best assumption is that the Studebaker management wished to concentrate on passenger cars.

The 1920's were the Golden Age for the Studebaker Corporation as it became recognized as a premiere manufacturer of automobiles and was very successful financially. Albert R. Erskine, the company president, was a very ambitious man both for himself and the corporation. He watched the developments at General Motors, the creation of the Chrysler Corporation, and the changes at the Ford Motor Company. Erskine wanted his company to run with the big boys and he devised a plan to be the only independent to convert from a single product manufacturer to a comprehensive full range manufacturer, which would jump Studebaker out of the independent group into an elite "Big Four."

Erskine's plan was based on a simple premise, Studebaker could make this jump by having a much larger product line. Of course, this would take money, but Erskine assumed that he had enough cash on hand. Some elements of this plan included the acquisition of Pierce-Arrow to give the company a high quality luxury car and a line of well respected heavy-duty trucks, the development of the Erskine and later the Rockne to compete in the low-priced automobile market, and the acquisition of The White Motor Company of Cleveland, Ohio, which had major truck lines in both the medium duty and heavy duty markets. How could the new Studebaker Corporation compete in the light-truck field? The answer was obvious and Studebaker re-

entered the commercial vehicle field in the 1927 model year with some light-duty models and several medium-duty models, but production was very low. Most trucks produced in the 1927 through 1930 model years were light-delivery vehicles based on automobile chassis. Sales were not strong, particularly as the model lineup did not include a pickup to compete with Chevrolet, Ford, GMC, Dodge or International. The new automotive conglomerate created a truck marketing company named S.P.A., Inc., which was responsible for sales of all trucks, including Autocar in some regions of the country. S.P.A. had products that covered all possible marketing niches in the medium and heavy duty commercial vehicle field.

During the first few years of the Great Depression, things did not go well for the Studebaker Corporation. The Erskine and Rockne cars failed to excite potential customers and eventually both lines were dropped. The year 1933 was difficult for Studebaker. President Erskine's disastrous policy of distributing millions of dollars in unearned dividends while the company fell further and further into debt led the company to seek receivership protection. The federal bankruptcy court appointed marketing vice president Paul G. Hoffman, production vice president Harold S. Vance and White Motor Chairman Ashton Bean as receivers. Erskine remained the nominal president, but he became both clinically depressed and personally insolvent. On July 1, 1933 Erskine killed himself. Both Pierce and White were sold off in 1934 to raise cash for the parent company.

During the years 1930 through 1935, Studebaker

concentrated on medium and heavy-duty vehicles, especially as the connections were broken between Studebaker, White, and Pierce. There were exceptions to this policy including the passenger car chassis that Studebaker sold to professional car coach makers during the years 1928 through 1940 for conversion into hearses, ambulances and funeral service cars, and the passenger car chassis sold to companies that installed station wagon bodies during the years 1933 through 1939. Consequently, most trucks sold by Studebaker during the years 1930 through 1936 were medium and heavy-duty units. The S series started in 1930, the T and W series in 1934, and a line of new Cab Forwards was introduced in 1936.

Not until 1937 did Studebaker return to the light-duty field, with the introduction of the J series and the Coupe-Express models. The latter a hybrid with Dictator passenger car styling in front and a durable commercial bed behind. The Coupe-Express was well styled as opposed to selling well, but it helped establish the Studebaker Corporation in the light duty field.

1937 was also noted for the first Studebaker diesel units. The K series was introduced in 1938 and continued through 1940. Coupe-Express models for the 1938 and 1939 years were based on Commander cars. In the 1940 model year, Studebaker produced a full range of medium and heavy-duty trucks, but no light-duty vehicles. One reason was the failure of the 1939 Coupe-Express to sell. Studebaker management, convinced they were on the wrong track by offering essentially a carlike truck, began planning for a truck that not only looked like a truck, but acted like a truck. This vehicle, however, would not be available in 1940.

I am indebted to Asa E. Hall, noted Studebaker historian and collector, who helped identify the vehicles and reviewed the introduction. The goal is a book as error free as possible.

1927 three-quarter-ton express car parked by factory.

1927 tow truck by factory.

1927 two-ton stake used for inter-factory freight on South Bend street.

1927 estate car.

1927 road washing unit mounted on cab and chassis photographed in factory yard.

1928 motor coach with Seminole body.

1928 refrigerated ice cream truck in Bloomington, Indiana.

1928 St. Louis, Missouri police paddy wagon.

1928 van inside custom body factory.

1928 enclosed van operated by National Biscuit Company.

1928 fire apparatus in full livery.

1928 Takoma Park, Maryland fire apparatus.

1928 special bodied tour bus.

1928 Blue Coach Lines motor bus by station.

1929 panel delivery used by *The Daily Star* on Toronto, Ontario streets.

1929 police patrol mounted on Commander chassis used in St. Catharines, Ontario.

1929 canvas topped van with extended cab produced for export.

1929 fire apparatus operated by Kamloops, British Columbia fire department.

1929 Studebaker Corporation photographic department truck on South Bend street.

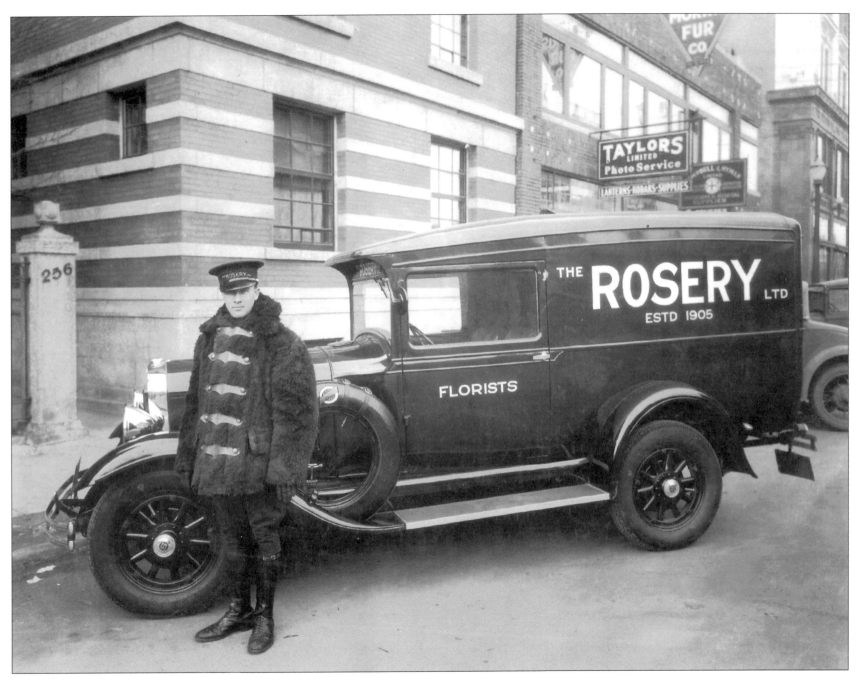

1929 wrecker unit mounted on truck chassis for Nu-Way Garage, Montreal, Quebec.

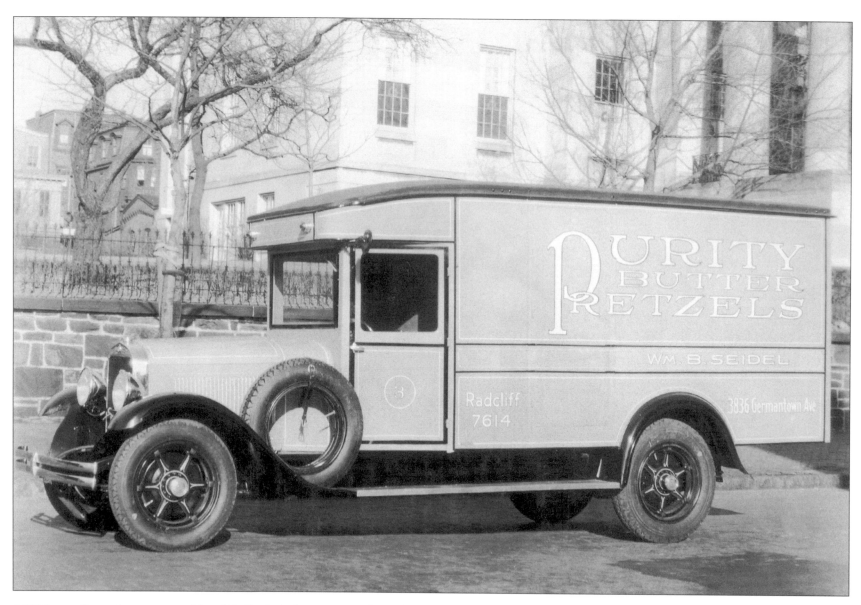

1929 enclosed van used by Philadelphia pretzel maker.

1929 panel delivery parked by truck factory.

Late 1920s Paramount Pictures camera cars and actress Jean Arthur.

Late 1920's Model 99 with LaFrance triple combination unit used by Trail, British Columbia fire department.

1930 stake bodied truck used by Toronto, Ontario oil distributor.

1930 three-quarter-ton panel delivery in Winnepeg, Manitoba.

1930 Two three-quarter-ton panel deliveries used by Regina, Saskatchewan cleaners.

1931 cab and chassis used by Chicago dealer to advertise new truck models.

1931 one-and-one-half-ton express operated by the Toronto Evening Telegram in Oakville, Ontario.

1931 one-and-one-half-ton express used by Philadelphia butcher.

1931 183-inch wheel base stake exported to Shanghai, China.

1931 enclosed van parked by Philadelphia mansion.

1931 and 1933 tractor trailer units used for fast freight work between South Bend and Chicago.

1934 T241 St. Louis, Missouri street department repair truck.

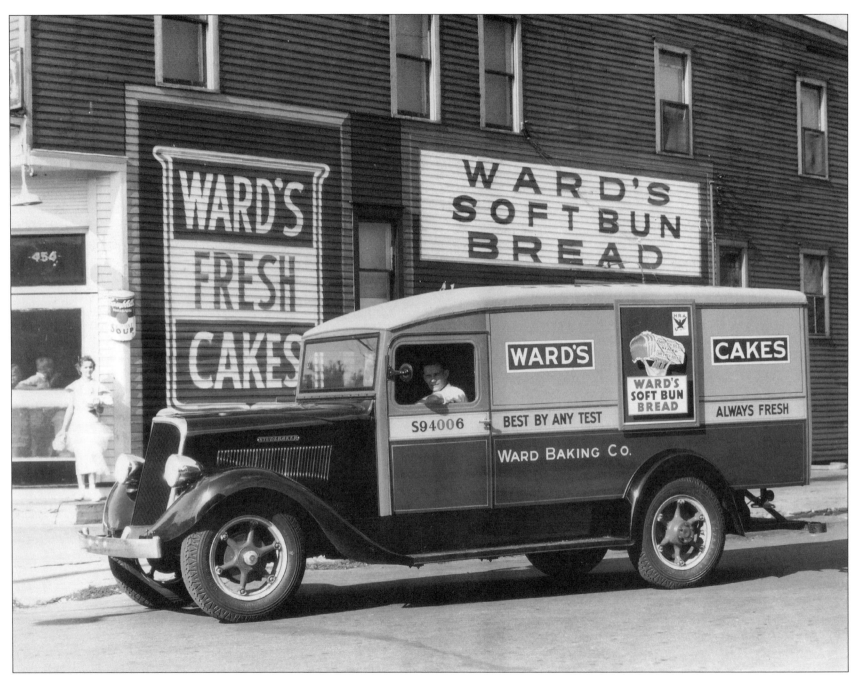

1934 one-and-one-half-ton van on Philadelphia street.

1934 enclosed van on Philadelphia street.

1934 T241 closed body truck by Richmond, Virginia warehouse.

1934 T665 enclosed van owned by Kendall Oil distributor in Utica, New York.

1934 oil tanker operated by Texaco distributor in Milton, Pennsylvania.

1934 refrigerated ice cream delivery unit operated by The Borden Company.

1934 T241 two-ton coal body with hoist on Newark, New Jersey street.

1934 T683 brewer's stake operated by Ebling's of New York City.

1934 wrecker operated by the Automobile Club of Portugal. Note the non-factory cab.

1934 T683 moving van used by Red Bank, New Jersey mover.

1934 T265 FitzJohn bus operated by the Chicago, South Bend and South Shore Railroad.

1934 Edwards sleeper cab tractor with Edwards trailer used for marketing demonstrations.

1934 T265 fire apparatus built by Leonhardt used by Jessup, Maryland fire department.

1934 Chief Heil dumper with hoist owned by Pipkorn Fuel and Supply Company, Oshkosh, Wisconsin.

1934 W865 triple combination fire apparatus used by Clayton, Delaware fire company.

1933 DeKalb step van body mounted on cab and chassis.

1933 T665 enclosed van operated by Grand Forks, North Dakota candy company.

1933 road oiling body mounted on cab and chassis.

1935 1W765 with Edwards stake body used by gas company in Chicago, Illinois.

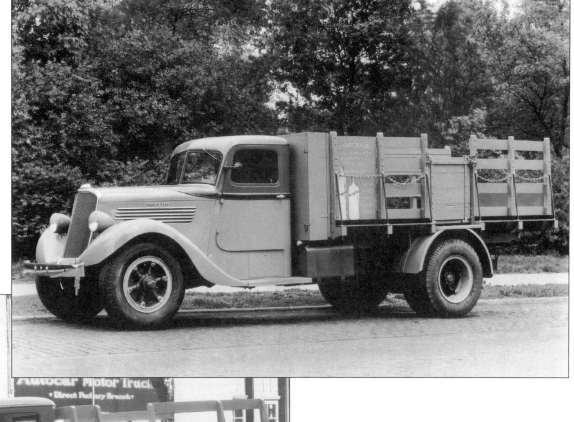

1935 1T241 special stake operated by St. Louis, Missouri gas company.

1935 1T683 enclosed van operated by Newark, New Jersey freight line.

1935 cowl and chassis fitted with special Railway Express bodies.

1935 Edwards sleeper cab with Edwards trailer on South Bend road.

1935 1W841 deluxe cab with Edwards trailer used by Newark, Ohio brewer photographed in front of Cincinnati Union Station.

1935 1W865 three-four ton dumper with 710 HP Waukesha engine on road building duty in Seattle, Washington.

1935 conventional cab tractor and trailer hauling Sir Malcolm Campbell's racer "Bluebird" at Canadian National Exhibition in Toronto, Ontario.

1935 1T265 Sanford equipped fire apparatus owned by the West Albany, New York fire department.

1935 1T241 deluxe service panel used by Autocar Branch in East Chicago, Illinois. Note extra cost Budd disc wheels.

1935 1T241 hydraulic hoist dumper operated by Cincinnati, Ohio building supply company.

1935 refrigerated unit used by Abbotts Dairies in Cameron, Wisconsin.

1936 Model 2T2 step van owned by
Portland, Oregon dairy.

1936 2M225 open van operated by
Phoenix, Arizona dairy.

1936 2W865 1000 gallon oil tanker operated by Sinclair Oil Company, Chicago, Illinois.

1936 Cities Service oil tanker at Wisconsin service station.

1936 American Oil Company tanker delivering oil to Syd Walke's service station.

1936 Two 2M625 units with concrete mixer bodies in Covington, Kentucky.

1936 2M201 combination stake and dumper operated by Buffalo, New York building supply company.

1936 2M257 lumber body used by Chicago, Illinois millwork company.

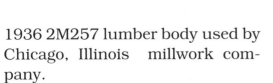

1936 Canvas topped van operated by wholesale grocer in Crawfordsville, Indiana.

1936 Cab forward unit operated by Victoriaville, Quebec furniture manufacturer.

1936 Two 2M225 and one 2M657 with Koback bodies operated by San Diego bottler.

1936 FitzJohn bodied 27 passenger bus operated by Tennessee bus company.

1936 2M601 tractor with moving van trailer used by Bekins Van Lines in San Francisco, California.

1936 Tractor with Fruehauf trailer operated by Detroit, Michigan brewery.

1936 Bromo Quinine demonstrator unit operated by the Grove Pharmaceutical Company.

1936 Standard Series three-quarter ton Chief tractor and trailer used for store deliveries by Red and White Stores, Walla Walla, Washington.

1936 2T257 fire apparatus delivered to Stillwater, Minnesota fire department.

1936 one-and-one-half-ton Edwards panel on South Bend street.

1936 2M225 cab forward coal body with hoist on Philadelphia street.

1937 J20 Edwards stake by truck factory building.

1937 J Stake truck used by chicken farmer.

1937 J15-38 Standard Series bread body owned by Ward Baking Company, South Bend, Indiana.

1937 J Bottler's rack operated by American Soda Water Company by St. Louis, Missouri tavern.

1937 J Wrecker operated by Modesto, California dealer.

1937 J15M with Batavia refrigerated body built for Fond du Lac, Wisconsin dairy.

1937 J30 coal dumper with hoist and California headlights parked by apartment house.

1937 J30M five-ton coal truck with hoist used in Brooklyn, New York.

1937 J25 Edwards dumper with California headlights.

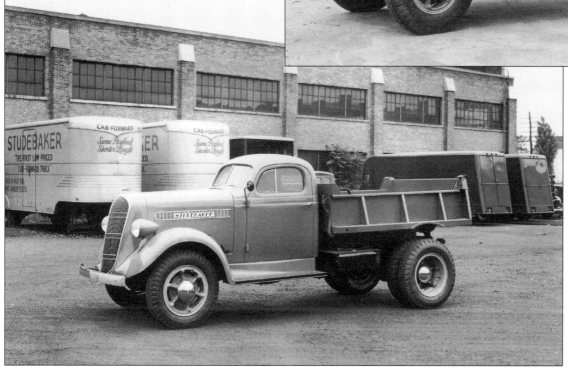

1937 J Edwards dumper in front of Studebaker Corporation's demonstration trailers.

1937 J American Oil Company tanker at Virginia station.

1937 J30M Richfield oil tanker at Philadelphia petroleum distributorship.

1937 J Cab Forward unit with special trailer at St. Louis, Missouri auto show.

1937 J Bus delivered for service in Salt Lake City, Utah.

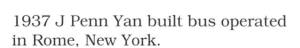

1937 J Penn Yan built bus operated in Rome, New York.

1937 J Fire apparatus delivered to Pennsylvania fire company.

1937 J5 Coupe-Express half-ton operated by Phoenix Brewery Corporation of Buffalo, New York.

1937 J15 Edwards panel in factory yard.

1938 K10 three-quarter or one-ton fast transport operated by Studebaker Corporation in South Bend.

1938 K10 Panel truck used by Studebaker's photographic department.

1938 K10 three-quarter to one-ton pickup.

1938 K10 three-quarter to one-ton Edwards stake parked by South Bend poultry market.

1938 K10 one-ton Edwards custom panel truck.

104

1938 K15 coal body with hydraulic hoist by Indiana coal yard.

1938 K stake owned by Canton, Ohio hardware company.

1938 K special stake bodied truck operated by Portland, Oregon Electrical Products Company.

1938 K15 furniture van parked by Studebaker and Packard dealer in Ashtabula, Ohio.

1938 K20 enclosed brewer's van used by Chicago Heights, Illinois beer distributor.

1938 K15 one-ton Montpelier urban panel truck.

1938 K15 one-ton urban panel truck operated by Ventura, California baker.

1938 K Refrigerated ice cream unit owned by Boise, Idaho dairy.

1938 K Cities Service oil tanker by art deco service station.

1938 K15-38 Holmes bodied wrecker in service in Mahanoy City, Pennsylvania.

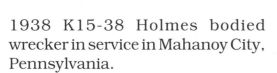

1938 K Garbage trucks delivered to City of Lorain, Ohio.

1938 K20 sleeper cab manufactured by Orville Body Company, Orville, Ohio.

1938 K25 fire apparatus, rated two-and-one-half to four-tons, delivered to Galveston, Texas fire department.

1938 K fire apparatus owned by Patterson Township fire company.

1938 K25-80 Crown 43 passenger bus owned by Ventura, California high school.

1938 K5 coupe-expresses owned by oil well service company.

1939 K5 coupe-express used for light-delivery by Dallas, Texas tire dealer.

1939 Studebaker truck display at the 1939 Chicago truck show.

1939 K series wrecker owned by Worcester, Massachusetts garage towing wrecked Hudson car.

1939 K series canvas topped cargo truck, of the type exported to the French, Dutch, and Belgian armies.

1940 K10-738 express used by Canton, Ohio electric company.

1940 K15F one-and-one-half-ton military truck prototype apparently not awarded a government contract. Notice dual wheels on right front.

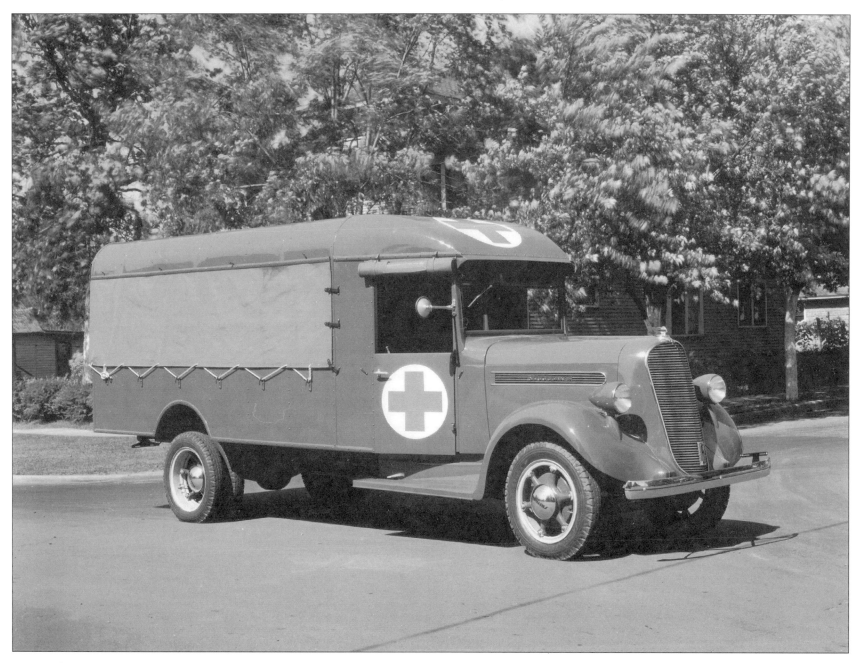

One of several 1940 K15 ambulances delivered to the Chinese Red Cross.

1940 K25MB Lattimore school bus featuring special California head lamps and photographed in San Francisco, California.

The photographs reproduced in this book are from many private and public collections. Many of these photographs were sent originally to newspapers at the beginning of model years in the hopes of free publication. Other photographs were created by body builders, automotive dealers, corporations, the US Army, and free-lance commercial photographers. Some of these photographs, as well as thousands of others of American passenger cars and commercial vehicles, are available at wholesale or retail. Studebaker truck and car original sales literature, owner manuals, tune-up charts, and paint charts also are available, as are similar materials for most popular American and foreign marques. Inquiries from buyers and sellers of automobilia are invited.

APPLEGATE AND APPLEGATE
BOX 260
ANNVILLE, PENNSYLVANIA 17003

EVENING TELEPHONE: (717) 964-2350

The Iconografix Photo Archive Series includes:

TRACTORS AND CONSTRUCTION EQUIPMENT

CASE TRACTORS 1912-1959 Photo Archive	ISBN 1-882256-32-8
CATERPILLAR MILITARY TRACTORS VOLUME 1 Photo Archive	ISBN 1-882256-16-6
CATERPILLAR MILITARY TRACTORS VOLUME 2 Photo Archive	ISBN 1-882256-17-4
CATERPILLAR SIXTY Photo Archive	ISBN 1-882256-05-0
CATERPILLAR THIRTY Photo Archive	ISBN 1-882256-04-2
FARMALL F-SERIES Photo Archive	ISBN 1-882256-02-6
FARMALL MODEL H Photo Archive	ISBN 1-882256-03-4
FARMALL MODEL M Photo Archive	ISBN 1-882256-15-8
FARMALL REGULAR Photo Archive	ISBN 1-882256-14-X
FORDSON 1917-1928 Photo Archive	ISBN 1-882256-33-6
HART-PARR Photo Archive	ISBN 1-882256-08-5
HOLT TRACTORS Photo Archive	ISBN 1-882256-10-7
JOHN DEERE MODEL A Photo Archive	ISBN 1-882256-12-3
JOHN DEERE MODEL B Photo Archive	ISBN 1-882256-01-8
JOHN DEERE MODEL D Photo Archive	ISBN 1-882256-00-X
JOHN DEERE 30 SERIES Photo Archive	ISBN 1-882256-13-1
MINNEAPOLIS-MOLINE U-SERIES Photo Archive	ISBN 1-882256-07-7
OLIVER TRACTORS Photo Archive	ISBN 1-882256-09-3
RUSSELL GRADERS Photo Archive	ISBN 1-882256-11-5
TWIN CITY TRACTOR Photo Archive	ISBN 1-882256-06-9

TRUCKS

DODGE TRUCKS 1929-1947 Photo Archive	ISBN 1-882256-36-0
DODGE TRUCKS 1948-1960 Photo Archive	ISBN 1-882256-37-9
MACK MODEL AB Photo Archive	ISBN 1-882256-18-2
MACK MODEL B 1953-66 Photo Archive	ISBN 1-882256-19-0
MACK MODEL B 1953-1966 VOLUME 2 Photo Archive	ISBN 1-882256-34-4
MACK EB, EC, ED, EE, EF, EG & DE 1936-1951 Photo Archive	ISBN 1-882256-29-8
MACK EH-EJ-EM-EQ-ER-ES 1936-1950 Photo Archive	ISBN 1-882256-39-5
MACK FC, FCSW & NW1936-1947 Photo Archive	ISBN 1-882256-28-X
MACK FG-FH-FJ-FK-FN-FP-FT-FW 1937-1950 Photo Archive	ISBN 1-882256-35-2
MACK LF-LH-LJ-LM-LT 1940-1956 Photo Archive	ISBN 1-882256-38-7
STUDEBAKER TRUCKS 1927-1940 Photo Archive	ISBN 1-882256-40-9
STUDEBAKER TRUCKS 1941-1964 Photo Archive	ISBN 1-882256-41-7

AUTOMOTIVE

AMERICAN SERVICE STATIONS 1935-1943 Photo Archive	ISBN 1-882256-27-1
IMPERIAL 1955-1963 Photo Archive	ISBN 1-882256-22-0
IMPERIAL 1964-1968 Photo Archive	ISBN 1-882256-23-9
LE MANS 1950: THE BRIGGS CUNNINGHAM CAMPAIGN Photo Archive	ISBN 1-882256-21-2
SEBRING 12-HOUR RACE 1970 Photo Archive	ISBN 1-882256-20-4
STUDEBAKER 1933-1942 Photo Archive	ISBN 1-882256-24-7
STUDEBAKER 1946-1958 Photo Archive	ISBN 1-882256-25-5

AVAILABLE EARLY 1996

CLETRAC AND OLIVER CRAWLERS Photo Archive	ISBN 1-882256-43-3
COCA-COLA: A HISTORY IN PHOTOGRAPHS 1930-1969	ISBN 1-882256-46-8
COCA-COLA: ITS VEHICLES IN PHOTOGRAPHS 1930-1969	ISBN 1-882256-00-X
FARMALL SUPER SERIES Photo Archive	ISBN 1-882256-49-2
INTERNATIONAL TRACTRACTORS Photo Archive	ISBN 1-882256-48-4
PACKARD 1935-1941 Photo Archive	ISBN 1-882256-44-1
PACKARD 1942-1958 Photo Archive	ISBN 1-882256-45-X
PHILLIPS 66 1945-1953 Photo Archive	ISBN 1-882256-42-5
SEBRING 12 HOUR RACE 1962 Photo Archive	ISBN 1-882256-51-4
SEBRING 12 HOUR RACE 1965 Photo Archive	ISBN 1-882256-50-6

The Iconografix Photo Archive Series is available from direct mail specialty book dealers and bookstores worldwide, or can be ordered from the publisher. For additional information or to add your name to our mailing list contact:

Iconografix
PO Box 609
Osceola, Wisconsin 54020 USA

Telephone: (715) 294-2792
(800) 289-3504 (USA and Canada)
Fax: (715) 294-3414

Book trade distribution by Voyageur Press, Inc. (800) 888-9653

IMPERIAL 1955-1963
PHOTO ARCHIVE

Edited by P. A. Letourneau

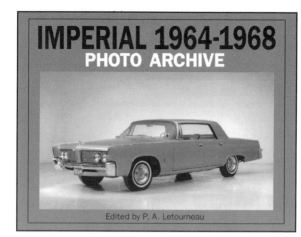

IMPERIAL 1964-1968
PHOTO ARCHIVE

Edited by P. A. Letourneau

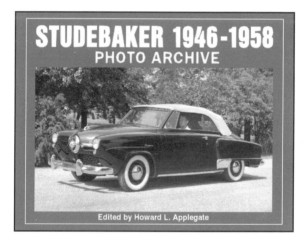

STUDEBAKER 1946-1958
PHOTO ARCHIVE

Edited by Howard L. Applegate

STUDEBAKER 1933-1942
PHOTO ARCHIVE

Edited by Howard L. Applegate

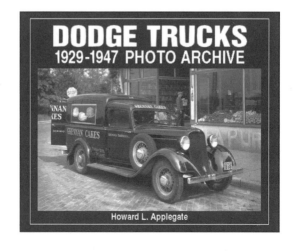

DODGE TRUCKS
1929-1947 PHOTO ARCHIVE

Howard L. Applegate

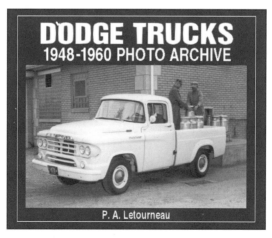

DODGE TRUCKS
1948-1960 PHOTO ARCHIVE

P. A. Letourneau

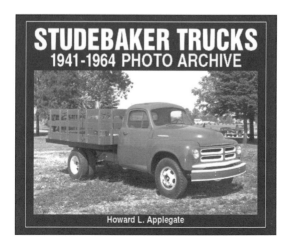

STUDEBAKER TRUCKS
1941-1964 PHOTO ARCHIVE

Howard L. Applegate